EXQUISITE
POLITICS

EXQUISITE POLITICS

Denise
Duhamel

Maureen
Seaton

TIA CHUCHA PRESS
CHICAGO

Grateful acknowledgment is made to the editors of the following publications where these poems first appeared:

Crab Orchard Review: "Exquisite Candidate," "Exquisite Politics"

Hanging Loose: "Suicide"

Jack Leg: "Beach Bunnies"

membrane: "A Crown of Spells to Ward off Susans," Nos. 2, 3, 5, 7

The Mid-American Review: "Ecofeminism in the Year 2000"

Poet Lore: "Let Me Explain"

Prairie Schooner: "Exquisite Incumbent," "Exquisite Independent," "Exquisite Majority," "Exquisite Minority"

Spoon River Poetry Review: "A Crown of Spells to Ward off Susans," Nos. 1,4, 6, "The Drag Queen's Wife," "The Femme Diaries"

two girls review: "Litany of the Fathers"

Special thanks to Janet Bloch, Mary Hawley, and Gregg Shapiro.
And special love to Jennie, Emily, Kerri, Kate, and Athena from both of us.

Printed in the United States of America

ISBN 1-882688-15-5
Library of Congress Number: 97-61748

Book design: Jane Brunette
Cover painting: *Ballerina Cowgirl* by Jeanette May,
© 1993, courtesy of Woman Made Gallery
Author photo: Jennifer and Emily Bowe
Project Manager: Mary Hawley

PUBLISHED BY:
TIA CHUCHA PRESS
A Project of the Guild Complex
PO Box 476969
Chicago, IL 60647

DISTRIBUTED BY:
NORTHWESTERN UNIVERSITY PRESS
Chicago Distribution Center
11030 S. Langley
Chicago, IL 60628

Funding for this project was partially provided by the National Endowment for the Arts, the Illinois Arts Council, and the Lannan Foundation.

For Nick
(D.D.)

For Lori
(M.S.)

Some say a host of cavalry or infantry
is the most beautiful sight
on the black earth, and some say
long ships; but I say
whomever one loves is.

SAPPHO

Man does not live by words alone,
despite the fact that sometimes
he has to eat them.

ADLAI STEVENSON

CONTENTS

INTRODUCTION

DENISE DUHAMEL: Maureen and I began to work seriously together in 1990. We didn't know what would come of our collaborations—if we would ever try to publish them or read them publicly. We were eager for experimentation with language, pushing beyond the level of our comfort zones. In the beginning, we agreed upon certain ground rules: at first we worked in syllabics and were not allowed to change anything about the other's lines, though we kept open the option of changing/adding/eliminating end punctuation in any given line that preceded the one we wrote; and we decided upon the number of lines before we began each poem. We chose loosely defined "topics" before we began, but our collaborative poems (like the poems we wrote individually) often grew to have lives of their own, ones we didn't expect.

MAUREEN SEATON: Together we undertook projects that were either really wild (witches' spell sonnets), emotionally challenging (our childhoods, ex-loves, etc.), or intellectually challenging (writing in forms, using rhyme schemes). We often pushed the limits of convention thematically. It seemed appropriate to be outrageous as a team because being a team is already outrageous, at least in some circles. It feels powerful. We write for women, for ourselves, my daughters, Denise's nieces. We're committed to women in our individual work but it's heightened when we collaborate. Sometimes consciously, sometimes not.

DUHAMEL: After six years of writing our collaborative poems, we were ready to assemble a book-length manuscript. As we looked at what we had, we realized much of the book was about politics—gender politics in particular. We began to write a series of "Exquisite Politics" poems, playing Exquisite Corpse, the surrealist parlor game where half the lines remain hidden until the end. Those poems were particularly fun since they took us out of ourselves and allowed us to write about politics in a very nonlinear way.

SEATON: Sometimes I struggle to perceive the identity(ies), voice(s) of our poems. At times the voices ring clearly and definably as either Denise's or mine. Other times there is only the one voice of the poem and ours are subsumed. That is what feels most spectacular about collaboration, that creation of a third person, but I'm not always objective enough to see/hear it. And then, lately, I'm not sure how important it really is to create the new voice. In *Exquisite Politics,* boundaries—including the boundaries of our own identities—are explored, blurred, obliterated, joined, all kinds of organic things.

DUHAMEL: Before working with Maureen, I'd had a few unsuccessful attempts at collaboration. I always tell people that Maureen is the only one who can keep up with me—that is, we have a lot of endurance. We've worked for month long periods during the summer, in a pretty much 9-5 fashion. We have also had a few long weekends doing not much else but writing and talking about writing. Collaboration has given me a sense of joy in working with another, Maureen, when I thought I was incapable of such work.

SEATON: I've often thought that both the desire and the ability to collaborate in our writing stand for something larger in our individual lives. Because the process of collaboration is such a vulnerable one (the potential blending of two individual voices and sensibilities), so intimate, it's provided countless metaphors for the larger picture. Denise and I enjoy working through the snags, and we delight in each other's words. There is an incredible pride and humility in signing both of our names to a piece of writing. It feels natural. And brave. We're not unaware that we're doing something "unusual," even taboo for women in our society.

It makes the process exciting. But it's incredibly hard work too. We've come through anger, fatigue, hurt feelings. The best of friends find some way to be a team, I think. The best of lovers do too.

DUHAMEL: A word of advice to would-be collaborators—it's imperative that you like being in the same room with each other for long stretches and that you both get hungry at the same time.

—D. D. & M. S., *New York & Chicago, May, 1997*

EXQUISITE CANDIDATE

I can promise you this: food in the White House
will change! No more granola, only fried eggs
flipped the way we like them. And ham ham ham!
Americans need ham! Nothing airy like debate for me!
Pigs will become the new symbol of glee,
displacing smiley faces and "Have A Nice Day."
Car bumpers are my billboards, billboards my movie screens.
Nothing I can say can be used against me.
My life flashes in front of my face daily.
Here's a snapshot of me as a baby. Then
marrying. My kids drink all their milk which helps
    the dairy industry.
A vote for me is not only a pat on the back for America!
A vote for me, my fellow Americans, is a vote for everyone
    like me!
If I were the type who made promises
I'd probably begin by saying: America,
relax! Buy big cars and tease your hair
as high as the Empire State Building.
Inch by inch, we're buying the world's sorrow.
Yeah, the world's sorrow, that's it!
The other side will have a lot to say about pork
but don't believe it! Their graphs are sloppy coloring books.
We're just fine—look at the way
everyone wants to speak English and live here!
Whatever you think of borders,
I am the only candidate to canoe over Niagara Falls

and live to photograph the Canadian side.
I'm the only Julliard graduate—
I will exhale beauty all across this great land
of pork rinds and gas stations and scientists working for cures,
of satellite dishes over Sparky's Bar & Grill, the ease
of breakfast in the mornings, quiet peace of sleep at night.

SUICIDE

He would leave the bar in Yonkers and walk the streets until daylight. Somehow, in the way known only to prostitutes, he would know how to look like he was for sale and he would know who to look for and he would know exactly where to walk to make all this possible, this selling of his flesh—in particular, the penis bent to the left or right when hard. The men would be pathetic he said, small and bald or full of pimples or very pudgy or they had a lisp or they had lots of money and nothing to do with it. He was always the one on top. He promised me this even before we'd heard of AIDS, he promised it with an air of superiority, as if taking in a penis is so much weaker than forcing it in. The men paid him and needed him and he was drunk and they were usually drunk and it was years ago although not that many years ago really because he was only two years sober when we met. He scared me with his stories although he never went into detail. He wasn't proud or not proud but still the stories existed and there were more to come that were scarier, like the times he'd be sober and pick up a gay guy in the village and just tease him. Through the break-up years, he liked to tell me these stories and why I listened I'll never know. It was a kind of exquisite torture he put me through, I think, to repay me for letting him down.

*

Two penises battle each other like soft swords, brush against each other at night—the bumping heads of two roughhousing

16

children. The penises spiral like the pharmacist's Rexall sign, like DNA, like mattress coils. They seem redundant at first until there are willing hands and mouths and darker holes.

*

When Jim was in sixth grade he had a crush on Mr. Dupont who stood in front of the board, all moustache and beard. The equations faded behind him as Jim wondered how many wonderful hairs he had on that face. What it would feel like to pet him, tenderly, like he petted his cats. Mr. Dupont wore plaid pants and big heavy shoes. Jim was too ashamed to stay after school, his grades worse and worse as the year went on, numbers strangling themselves in his head.

*

I think about him thinking about Steven as I danced in his mother's antique slip, trying to seduce him after our fight. Another time he refused to leave my bed. When I tried to kick him out he held on to the mattress crying. When I came back from my walk he was still there in the same position. Not that this proves love. Not that this proves anything. He took a picture of me once, just my legs. He brushed my hair and held my hand.

*

My friend Winnie was too fat to have sex or even a boyfriend. She lived with Jim on Broadway in Yonkers. They fixed up the apartment like husband and wife. They cooked expensive dinners and ate together, though he was often late as husbands are. He complimented her clothes and hair, the way she arranged fresh flowers. Then on her birthday he hired a male prostitute so she could lose her virginity. She was thirty. She'd never taken her clothes off in front of anyone. Her thighs were as wide as the pillows on the couch. She cried and the prostitute wound up stripping for her instead and saying goodnight. He later snuck into Jim's bedroom where the two of them had sex. They opened like fault lines. They shook the bed. Winnie didn't even have a vibrator, her mysterious clitoris hidden somewhere in the folds of all that flesh. She went to gay bars and when she was drunk tried to kiss the men. One poured beer over her head. Buster was into bondage and drugs. His roommate often came home to find him naked, tied to a chair. He was shot at when he owed money. He had a beard like a TV cop. Winnie loved him. He said he'd done women, but only doggie style.

*

The woman was in the right-hand corner of my dream and the child (a girl, about 8) was in the left-hand corner. The woman flew to the ceiling, her legs kind of crooked behind her and shrunken, actually. She kind of became a huge bird and flew over to her daughter who was miraculously hidden from my sight by something resembling a church pew. Miraculously because the woman was holding a giant block of cement, and as she landed beside the girl began beating her with her strange weapon. The child's battered face became visible. Now she was sitting in a pew with other children, and the audience in my dream said "Oh" in shock and sadness.

*

This is what I imagine for him: Always wrestling with his chubbiness. Fussing over his hair. He didn't mind being used, in fact, welcomed it. It frightened me, the way people could use him up, and I wonder how I used him, if I did, and if I held the gun and pulled the trigger.

*

When I was sleeping with Jim he told me that he'd been with a man who lived in New York City. We met at the gallery. I knew it was him, as Jim touched his arm the same way he touched mine. The man was shorter than I was, Japanese, with delicate features. I felt jealous, as though he were prettier, as though he might have more interesting things to say than I would, standing there with a diet coke in his hand, the yellow and green painting

18

behind his head. Jim wanted everyone: the waitress with forty
earrings up her lobe, the man who sold him liquor at the corner
store. What would it be like if they were in bed with us now?
Where would you touch them? I played along because I didn't
know what else to do. He was wearing my fish net tights. Regular
sex wasn't enough. What did you do with the man? I wanted to
know. I fucked him. He said it was like having capers on the
side, something he only had a taste for once in a while.

*

Winnie and Jim would walk from the cowboy bar to the Korean
grocers, drunk and pointing at dusty blue cans of shredded
coconut. No one in the East Village had made Piña Coladas in
such a long time. It was funny—that palm tree on the can, that
sugar in the mixture that made Winnie want to buy it and eat it
by the spoonfuls like ice cream. She was there because she'd
waited all those years for a boyfriend. You couldn't bring Jim
home to your mom, but at least he never made fun of the fat. He
played with the flab under her arm while he was talking about
stars colliding, strange science. He had a computer with a black
screen and white letters. Winnie watched him work, before him a
small window on the night sky.

*

Winnie was scared when they rented the car and drove to
Canada. Jim drank beer and mooed out the windows at the cows.
He took Winnie on a hike through the woods, making her walk
ahead at the beginning so he could watch her ass move. He
quickly passed her up the hill. She was out of breath and broke
out in a sweat. She wasn't sure which way was the way back to
the car, Jim zigzagging through the evergreens and pines,
ignoring the trails which were clearly marked. By now she wasn't
even on a trail. Her feet slipped on wet rocks, her thighs rubbed
against each other, the hem of her shorts inching towards her
crotch. She hated Jim, she told the sky, each crunchy acorn. She
wanted to lie down and die, imagined a rescue team finding her
blue and bloated. A police officer would call her parents who

would say, "Where was Mary?" (She told them she was going away with her girlfriend.) When Winnie finally found Jim he was lounging naked on a huge rock, his clothes littered around the pine needles. Her face was scratched and sore, she'd walked into so many branches. She threw a handful of pebbles at him but missed.

*

Jim told me about his mother: When he was little she held him down on the floor with her knee and punched him in the ear. Punctured his eardrum. When I first met her she looked at me with sadness as if to say: I didn't mean to but I fucked this one up.

*

Some days he imagined himself as lady-killer James Dean, other days he was Kerouac searching for his Cassady. He drove his truck out into the middle of a golf course and ran a hose from the tail pipe into the cab. He made sure no one would find him—no ritual garage, no note—but the grounds keeper came along and saved his life. Every June he'd threaten suicide. He said he couldn't bear the thought of another summer. His eyes were the goddamnest blue I'd ever seen and when I would look into them it was as if they were the top of a well deeper than anywhere.

*

Winnie and I were like ex-wives of the same dead man. Winnie smoked slowly and talked slowly, sometimes for hours without interruption. She loved thin seaweed crackers and small delicate knickknacks. Another friend had recently died and her address book was full of Magic Marker blotches. No one loved her, she was sure of that. Her parents wanted her home for Christmas as if there could ever be a Christmas without Jim.

*

The first time we made love he chewed his lower lip as if the act required tremendous concentration. If the horses went wild after that, it was Jim who rode them across the finish line. When my mind was white light and my body acoustic, I'd feel afraid and not know why. He said: Let's imagine your friend Winnie in bed with us. Or John and Sheila. One by one he fantasy-fucked my friends until I disappeared up my own vagina and then I left him. He waited until June to die. He was 37 years old. I never made it to the funeral.

EXQUISITE MAJORITY

It's hard for me to get a good job.
I want a house, Nordic Track, and a new PC.
Sometimes I wonder about the word *consequences*.
I mean, nothing runs in a straight line, right?
I put on a shirt that says *Made in Japan*,
not on the label, but on the front. *Model Minority,*
Ms. X, Mr. X, Baby X American.
Non-nuclear and cut from nobody's mold.
If I were just a squiggle outline,
what color would I be? If I had sex with you,
would we smoke afterward? I worry about designer
clothes and my investment in American individuality.
(Tommy Hilfiger is the choice of certain gang-
members wearing two jackets at once to show off
their money. If I had to give my opinion,
I'd say—let the best designer win, man.)
If you're the only one in first grade with crooked bangs
I guess that makes you a minority, sort of.
Or answer this: If all the animals in the world died,
what the hell would we eat?
Yesterday I saw Nell Carter on Prince Street.
I'm a New Yorker so I didn't stare.
I walked down the steps to the six train,
slid my token into the slot.
A silver bar twirled and let me in.

LET ME EXPLAIN

It was easy for Jim to take off his clothes,
his body firm as a futon, his penis
just the right size. The small towel fit around his waist
perfectly, covered everything. I, on the other hand,
had all this flesh to worry about, breast to pubis—
lumpy thighs, thick ankles, the largest ass
at "Plato's Retreat."

What feels good on flesh?
Fringe on a book mark. Tassels on a graduation cap.
Cold metal coins in summer.

My grandmother pushes out her false teeth to make us laugh.
She is so sad, her husband dead so many years,
her children nothing but disappointment.
When I sleep with her, I rub my feet all up her legs.
I am so little. Her legs are so strong. I dive down to touch her toes.

When I want a massage, Jim says yes.
I pretend to sleep—otherwise it ends up sex. Once,
a woman rubbed my back and I cried after she left.
My body was a shaved bear, cold and prickly.

What is bisexual? Would I still love Jim
if he were a woman? Would I embrace his vulva gladly,
his soft breasts with nipples as sweet as hard candy?

My best friend is Carole Jenkins.
She wears pants to first grade and carries me on her back
up the steep cobblestone hill when my asthma flares.
She gets bad grades, gets into scrapes. I love her
like my teenage cousins love James Dean. She's arrested

in a bar brawl years later, taken to emergency for stitches
    over her eye.
Carole has a girlfriend with false eyelashes and costume jewelry
who cries when Carole is thrown the book, cries
at all those black stitches, a lost game of tic-tac-toe.
I go to court to tell of the time my tongue stuck
to the icy fence at recess. How Carole ran to get warm water
to separate my tongue from the fence like a Band-Aid from flesh.

What stops the bisexual from taking over the world,
sleeping with the boss, the boss's husband, the boss's Doberman?
It's not safe, all this nondiscriminatory salivation.
It's unsanitary, not neat.

I was ok when she touched me—not too terrified
and Jim was kind to me, tender as a new father.
She had cool fingers, respectful. At first I thought it was Jim,
but he was in me, busy with stronger mechanics.
She was blonde and white marble,
older, so her skin had begun that velvet stage.
Her husband was a shadow behind her.

Susan is a woman who wants everyone—
all at once, on every side, as if she is a room with no corners.
There is no one she won't fuck. There is no one
she can't take in her mouth and level in five minutes.

Susan came on to me. I told her I liked Jim.
She laughed and then slept with him.
Now I hate Susan, the way she twirls her long hair
    through dinner,
the way she sits too close to men and women,
that split down a couple, an ax through wood.

"I can fuck you, I can fuck your husband."
Someone who doesn't know diamonds from fakes.

God is hard on the bisexual woman—
a scornful subject for poetry.
God shakes his head at the woman
who loves whatever is there in front of her—
a chair, a cloud, a cheap wedding trinket.

There were small rooms big enough for a mattress
and four colliding bodies. My skin
was its own tight boundary, the air around me cheddar-sharp.
She was the light in our midst—plump lamb and halo.
I crossed over to her while my mind would let me,
while the angel of scent and glut perched on my tongue.
The men were busy with their eyes and hands,
their paternal regard. We were busy leaving them.

EXQUISITE MINORITY

When the stock market opened you could get
a really good steak dinner for three dollars—
one that would cost you sixty now.
Clout costs me: leg cramps, disc problems,
something around my heart they call dyspepsia.
I eat things bigger than I am but their brains are smaller.
Sheep, for instance, and cows.
In summer I pick mushrooms in France,
pay four hundred an ounce for the muskiest ones.
I like things that smell good—women,
barbecued beef. I once kissed a pig,
but I will not endure poverty.
As a child I chose the shoe in Monopoly.
I filled the Game of Life cars with pastel peg children
and went to jail then broke free. I got rich
on AT&T, Standard Oil, Mattel—
the best American in Englewood, New Jersey.
Most days, I'm nice to the maid
who irons the sheets just like my mom did.
I sweat in Armani, give me a break!
I'm realistic about money, power, taxes.
Of course, I'd like to be on TV.
I'd tell jokes to Letterman.
He'd laugh like a dad and invite me back.

THE DRAG QUEEN'S WIFE

1.

My husband Ming sang torch songs at our wedding
and people clapped like they were at a concert. The old uncles
were amazed when she took a break and went into
    the men's room.

Ming's got blue socks that light up her feet.
They cover her ankles, then there's a patch of skin
before the striped pajama legs.

Once we smashed raw eggs against the wall in Harlem.
There was no cleaning that mess, ever.
A kind of warped *Fantasia* followed, all those personified
    pots and pans.

The tambourines began playing themselves.
There were musical notes flying around the kitchen.
The treble clef stuck to the refrigerator

like a magnet. I was both repulsed and attracted.
I couldn't help it. I behaved like a Scales of Justice.
Blindfolded, breaking for lunch.

2.

What I don't know about drag queens could fill a book—
no, make that a set of encyclopedias, a *CD* set of encyclopedias.
The best computers are the reliable ones, the ones made to last

before the sixties. Ming's computer has a beehive. Mine's
into grunge and never dusts itself.
My parents can't believe I married Ming. They say,

"Your sister's normal, what happened to you?"
My vibrator's called Ms. Silky Smooth—
she's mauve and shiny like a hybrid fruit. Mauve—

now there's a beacon of changing fashion.
I remember when "artichoke" controlled the homes of America.
Ming calls her stove "avocado," says,

"Remember suburb brown?"—our mother's kitchens dark
and sorrowful? One corner in particular called the naughty
corner. It was where we had to stay if we were
    bad enough to smack.

3.

I'm tired of drag queens, I'm tired of push-up bras,
I'm tired of sitting in the tub until my skin melts off.
I'm tired of Ming saying oatmeal soap is good for me.

My finger pads wrinkle like wizened men.
My wrists wrinkle like bangle bracelets or tribal tattoos.
When Ming's ready, she'll tattoo a flower on my knee,

but first she has to study the begonia in our garden
and clean her needles. Ming brings a finger to her lips.
She needs me to quiet down but I can't.

I've waited for this tattoo my whole life—
now I fear it's lopsided. My kneecap flexes
and the petals disappear. I'm not bleeding since May.

Two more months and Baby Ming will steal the show.
I still dream about bleeding though
and sanitary napkins too tiny to prevent spills.

4.

The problem with our "same-sex" marriage is sex.
This, however, is not the only problem.
There's mold in the cupboard, ice

mounting in the freezer. Chemistry
exists into infinity, sparks along the continuum, but only
for some. Otherwise, it's over in a year.

The goddess of hypothalamus says: *Never mind the seasons—
let's get to work!* I make a broom from scratch,
sweep up my life and start fresh.

The first thing I decide to do is bungee jump.
I fiddle with the cords as I look down the drop
then hold my breath as I fly. It's like the dream

where I was Wendy and Peter Pan was my first "boyfriend,"
I followed her down Main Street—she was in black sequins,
I smoked a pipe. I couldn't ever be sure what it meant.

WHAT ARE HOMOSEXUALS FOR?

(AFTER ANDREW SULLIVAN'S *VIRTUALLY NORMAL*)

I used to think homosexuals were for comparisons, like: Here is my husband, the jock-itchy poker player. Here is the homosexual all dressed up at the ballet. Here is my husband, the last one off the commuter train with a beer buzz, newsprint smearing his cheek, grinning for his supper like Fred Flintstone after he was a bad boy. Here is the homosexual sprinting from his yellow convertible, the back seat stacked with library books—Jane Austen, Thomas Hardy—every hair in place as he kisses my hand and offers me a Gauloise. The homosexual wins in the best categories: sensitivity, gallantry, sophisticated humor. He understands me, even menstrual stuff fascinates him, he imagines the blood, creeping down his leg like a blessed initiation.

*

Homosexuals are for population control according to Andrew Sullivan. They're like the mule or some strange species found in the Galapagos Islands—how freely they have sex without worrying about pregnancy, how sadly they have sex knowing their limitations. Sullivan says gays make good nuns and school teachers. When Steven caught his brother trying on mascara, neither of them flinched. *Haven't you always wanted to try it?* he said and Steven took the wand in his hand like a princess. When Rae puts on a dress she says she's in drag, even though she's a woman the panty hose feel like a space suit. Then, of course, there are the straight men who dress in their wives' clothes and look like

matrons or twins if their wives join them. So what makes a homo-
sexual that different? I know a gay man who loves John Wayne
and cattle, who hates other gay men and has a wife and a daugh-
ter. I know a lesbian who dresses in lingerie and poses in men's
magazines. When I want to wear a disguise there is nothing in my
closet that feels right.

*

There are many classifications of homosexuals. Let's analyze what
femmes are for. First, the female femmes, or the homosexuals
who identify as females and also have female body parts. Like
me. Let's analyze me. I'm here for no apparent reason I can safely
say is true or God-given or necessary except that at some point,
all the seeds hit the land and I flew up, a girl-child, inside and
out, with a knack at vulnerability and a great need to be fucked
hard and long and lovingly. Same as some other femmes who
identify as female and have the body parts of men. The ones
called "swishy" or "queens," the ones who fly around in their
tutus, like me at age five on the stage of Miss Parlay's Ballet
School. We are pure yin. There is something so devastatingly soft
about us, America's eyes widen in disbelief. The straight man
yells obscene football things and the mom is afraid she overpro-
tected her son, and the father fantasizes, he can't help it, about
his daughter in bed with his mistress. Homosexuals used to be
for secrets. The country needed a huge vault of secrets. Pluto, the
farthest away darkest most secretive of planets, ruled the land
like the essence of every Pope. Now the homos peek into the
light like the first Johnny-jump-ups of spring. Let's analyze butch.

*

Butches are the ones who identify with men or sometimes they
identify with women and men, but chances are they think of
strapping on a penis and sticking it somewhere or they love to
use their natural-born penis to sink into the softness of the
femme. This, however, is not all they're for, and it's a great
mistake to think otherwise. Butch men pass in society as straight

31

guys so they are kind of cool for infiltration, getting to know you, if you're a woman heterosexual, you may fall easily in love and feel bitter for the rest of your life, looking for that gentleness you crave in the men who are bounding like Bambi around you, never quite dignifying the term *man*. Butch women, on the other hand, stand out like the combinations they are, that protean blend that any wise society (as in Native) would welcome, even raise up in some special way to be shamans or priest/esses. The butches who have big breasts are the most immortal of all God's children, they're for everything you could possibly think of to do with a man or a woman. They're delicious boundary walkers, they're the ones you need to take on night runs with their illegal knives cutting into their lovely butch thighs. They're the ones who will yell if an intruder comes to your door. They're muscle-y and their fingers are at the end of their muscles to heal you. Basically, butches are for femmes.

*

Fashion and pop songs. Dinner theater and good jokes. Where I grew up, there's now a group for gay high schoolers, can you believe it? I saw it on MTV, Tabitha Soren behind a map with a pin pointing into the belly of Rhode Island. When I was growing up all the so-called "fags" were my friends. Some didn't even know they were gay then. But Rob and Rick were like twins, kissing behind the white leatherette couch at a party in the projects. They chummed around in school like two girls, visiting each other's lockers and licking each other's ice cream sandwiches, squeezing out the vanilla so that it not only came out the sides but through the holes of the soggy cookie. It was obscene, let's face it, and they were beaten up. I held Brenda's hand and ran down the hall after drama rehearsal singing, "We are lesbians." We kissed each other's noses. The dykey gym teacher emerged from her red sports car and the roof of the car seemed to only reach her ankles. She was taller than the basketball hoop which Brenda could jump up and swing from while I watched, a femme in the stands. Lesbians weren't as fun as gay guys, we learned then, because we always had to be angry about women's issues and our periods and body image problems. But still we knew a thing or two about under-aged drinking and staying up all night to hear a radio interview of Elton John on a Providence station at four in the morning.

*

Rodney was in love with a Filipino man named Mario. I sat next to him at the funeral. He was there to take care of Rodney in the end, a nurse of sorts taking the ferry from Staten Island to St. Vincent's. Rodney had told me his boyfriend was still in the closet so I knew not to say too much when I hugged him during the "peace be with you" pause in the Mass. I wanted to say "I know you though we've never met." But Mario's parents were there, his mother in a dress so shiny and blue it reminded me of foil wrapping paper, his father stoic and a bit confused. Mario was hunched over and heaving, there for all of us to put a face on our grief. His was a secret so big we were afraid the world would shatter if we said "Rodney loved you. He told us all the time" and Mario's parents overheard. They would bring him home to punish him in some way that parents can punish adult children—probably by instilling guilt. I knew what homosexuals in the nineties were for—those sadly dutiful worker ants employed as pallbearers.

*

What are girl homos for? The first time I ever saw a lesbian I was an undergrad in a Catholic women's school. We had two, that's all, fric and fric-er, dour and dour-er, the unluckiest girls in school. They were for darkening up the campus with their sadness and undistinguished college careers. I never shared a sidewalk with them when they walked together, they never walked alone, and the little cloud that followed them from class to class, the swarm of bugs and dirt and gossip and stupidity, reminded me of Pigpen, and homosexuals are for making every-one else feel better about their misdemeanors. I used to drink booze then jump from my dorm window to meet the boys and drive recklessly through New Rochelle. I took down my panties eventually to the bartender I married in a fog of gin. I hated our two bodies the way we were taught the devil hates humankind, I hated our bodies so much I never let him touch me. I never touched him. We were holy spirits in a king-sized bed, holy and hetero, there was nothing in the way of our path to heaven and we knew it. We counted on it. It was all we ever had.

*

If I were a lesbian I could avoid that sperm ever spilling into me, all those cells multiplying into small spongy shapes and then a kid. If I were a lesbian I would not be my mother. I could escape giving little Junior a backhand, locking myself in my room with pills. If I were a lesbian I'd get lots of hugs, if not much sex, since I couldn't picture sex really except soft breasts falling over each other in sleep. But when I imagined "her" she was in her granny skirt, making me tea, her index finger holding up a tissue to dab away my crying so I wouldn't get wrinkles. I was so happy as we went shopping together and ate healthy snacks, but then I grew bored and saw a beard or muscled arm or a cold eye and my fantasy flew to other waters. And I knew that famous feminist was right—all straight women are masochists.

*

Sometimes I think homosexuals were created for a look at the divine looking at itself, that narcissistic plunge into the cool well, it's true, imagine loving yourself so much you materialize, you're a double now, when you take a look, there's your penis pointing back, there's your vulva perking up at your sly touch. The verb *bliss*. Sometimes I think homosexuals slipped in to take the heat off everyone else. One meaning of scapegoat I like is: the one in the family who knows the truth. But homosexuals are so human when you get to know them, so racist, sexist and homophobic, like everyone else, it's hard to accept this definition, unless, of course, the homosexual who knows the truth happens to be me, looking instead of falling into the well. There's America looking back, ready to enroll me in therapy or church or Scapegoats Anonymous. What is America for, I ask myself, then, like any good scapegoat, I run for my life.

EXQUISITE INDEPENDENT

Politics comes along when you least expect it.
It hides inside stories and fairy tales, fucking with the princess
who won't cry sexual harassment.
Its TV face is big and pink and puffy,
not the mother-loved face we all voted for.
Singular or plural, politics is/are unavoidable
in the womb and schoolyard and parking lot.
I once read a book called *How Things Work*.
I memorized Debussy's "Jimbo's Lullaby" for two hands,
the elephant who ran, remarkably, for king of the zoo.
I myself vote strictly independent—
writing in names like John Candy or Selena.
Now I'm heading towards re-naming parties—
thin and crispy for Democrats, pan pizza for Republicans.
The people will build a treehouse in each satellite dish
and wait for Santa Claus to knock door-to-door.

XENA: WARRIOR PRINCESS

I run through the muck of New Zealand
side-kicking fiends. Sword-fighting demons
add to the quackery of my even-
tempered sidekick's medical practice.
I'm good with a sword and herbal poultices
to cure my own wounds. Don't mistake my bruises
for mistakes. Every one was destined to boost
TV ratings and jolt the audience
from microwave popcorn and frozen fish sticks.
You can be me for Halloween. In fact,
I come in all cultures now, scratch
my surface, I'm complete as Barbra Streisand.
She can keep her press-on nails, her dopey fans.
I have warrior work to do, silvery plans.

THE FEMME DIARIES

1.

The femme is drinking from the art-deco glass.

That's her favorite time in history—before she lost her virginity,
before she lost it again to a girl.

She was open as a dolphin then, rubbing against
anything that felt good: sleeping bags, grandma, feather pillows.

Some butches think femmes are wimps, lazy, infantile.
Some femmes think the same of butches.
Some women deny they're butch or femme.

But you can imagine waking up male and female
    at the same time.

Or can you?

2.

The femme is looking at her pink TV.
She thinks there is nothing funnier than *I Love Lucy*.

Femme sounds so French, doesn't it? Like *crepes*
or *flambeau*. Butch sounds so bulldoggish or freckled

like one of the *Our Gang* kids or one of the Lost Boys.

If I were butch I'd probably wind up reading Robert Bly,
banging a drum in the woods on a wilderness weekend.

I thought I felt something like a penis enter me.
The pink flesh rose like a hairless cat.

You could burn yourself on my skin.

You could lose your reputation in my bouquet.

Not every femme wants flowers, especially when
    the butch buys them
with money from the femme's pocket.

3.

If I were a butch I'd have bigger feet.

My hips would look like parallel lines.
In a French film the man was attracted to women who looked
    like little boys.
It upset me, my thighs spread before me under my
    popcorn bucket.

Whatever they were showing on the screen had nothing
    to do with me.
I had to make my life up until I could find a woman
    and love her.

It was harder than it sounds. I owned a book called
    30 Master Plots.
In some cases you could guess who was who.
In my case that was impossible, even inadvisable.

I was a femme without a recipe book.

I was a butch without my supper before me.

4.

The butch said, "Take it from someone who doesn't have a clue."
The femme did—the advice as ill-fitting as a big sweater
   under a small coat.
If there was something sordid around, she would attract it.

Thus, along came a girl named Sam—big ears, small
breasts, all macho'd-out like David Lee Roth.
How could she not give her heart?

The femme giggled more than usual, like a rich princess.
The butch was sure she'd rather return to frog-dom.

So she gave the femme warts for words and crapped
   in the femme's hand.

So much for happy royalty.

The femme wished for a different kind of prince,
but the same ogres kept crossing her moat.

Finally, she swooned and was carried away to Manhattan
by a pigeon named Phoebe.

And they lived happily ever after, going back and forth
on the Staten Island Ferry. The End.

5.

Now the femme is cleaning the bathroom.

She leans over the tub, scouring, until sweat dots her hairline.
Will I ever be scrubbed enough to sit at the vanity
of all that is female? I shaved my legs, just to the knee

then wore knee-socks during sex.

Imagine hidden skin atrophying like a melon or growing hard
    as petrified wood,
the twin skeletons of your mom and dad
without apron or tool box to tell them apart.

That reminds me of the sitcom where the macho husband
expressed himself in pig-sounds and the wife
    was saintly indulgent.
She knew it wasn't nice to call her husband names.
Besides, then he pouted and wanted even more from her.

She called him her baby sometimes but it wasn't true.
He was everyone's baby.

Isn't it just like a femme to lose her whole poem to a man?
The fire stirs somewhere above her vagina, like a sacred heart.

6.

All the girl saints were femmes, except for Joan of Arc.

It's weird, isn't it, how you can't tell the difference between a
clothed baby boy or girl? Androgyny was the rage in the early
    eighties.

Until the energy polarized and settled itself again
into yin and yang, anima, animus. Coupling you can sink
    your teeth into.

It's like learning about magnets and batteries,
the upholstery of lust plumped up with orange foam.

Nothing says the femme can't initiate sex.

Nothing says the butch can't receive.

Once the butch came, rubbing against the femme's thigh
    until her bruises

were as dark as the night before Christmas.
Once I carried a cord of wood to the fireplace.
I watched my fire until the coals were abandoned cities.

7.

When a butch gets old is she called distinguished?
It's hard for the aging femme, hard on her estrogen.
Butches have it easy. On them,
aging looks good—even extra weight adds character.

The femme puts potpourri in bowls,
wears glasses with lenses that turn down so she can see
    to apply her mascara.

Still, she is embarrassed by Olive Oyl,

how she trots around on her rubbery legs saying,
    Popeye! Popeye!
Remember *Bewitched?* Samantha's butchy mother?
She was Tabitha's grandmother *and* grandfather.

If we were all naked and equal would the femmes
still put flowers in their hair?

You can always count on femmes and butches to
    confuse the hell out of you.
They count on each other for the exact same thing.

8.

What is it about a butch that makes everyone look at her?

Femmes have it easy, no telltale glint in the eye.
They play with sparkles and glue as little girls.
If they're lucky they're cheerleaders, or at least
    have good haircuts.

But sometimes a femme breaks from the herd. Nothing, she says,
   can stop me!
That's how I came to meet Betty.
She wore a shirt covered with embroidered spaceships.
She was so soft around the edges—how could I not love her?

She was all the essences of garden and continuum,
the flower being filmed opening backwards,
every other petal a butch then a femme.

EXQUISITE INCUMBENT

I'm here like a wife you've grown used to—
you like her casseroles, her dumb blonde jokes.
I'll never forget the secret entrance to the wine cellars,
how all along the way were footprints of past presidents.
Remember when Richard Nixon wore black socks
on the beach? Big mistake. I avoid caffeine and weak handshakes,
but I'm often lulled by my hopeless popularity,
the time it takes to call my limo to meet me at the back door.
I've held so many babies I feel like a nanny who wants to retire.
My smile is measured not to show too much gum.
Every tooth I've kept is a memorial to every unselfish political act,
every time I've asked myself: What about my country?
Then I feel bad about hearing the word "cunt"
inside country. I'm a pimp of my own people,
a ghostly duplicate of G.W. as he crossed the Delaware
in search of one more vote, one more chance to win.
I'm Henry VIII waiting for his own beheading.
Fix me a good stiff drink—I'll need it
as I study the graphs, the big chunk of voters
leaning towards the new kid on the block,
the new boy from California with his sun-drenched hair,
his cool three-wheeler and the tribal tattoo.
As an incumbent, it's not a good idea for me to endorse anything
though there'll be the book deal and speaking tour
if this doesn't work out. Like Stephen King I'll only read
at independent bookstores. Or I'll sell stuff on TV
like Joe Namath or Frank Gifford. I'd like to open

my own restaurant
and serve all the foods they made fun of me for eating—
seaweed, ovaltine, beef marrow sucked right from the bone.
Que sera sera, my fellow Americans.
When I was just a little boy, I asked my mother nothing
and went ahead, up ladders, over rooftops, and look where I am.

A CROWN OF SPELLS TO WARD OFF SUSANS

1.

Stop crying. Bring all her costume jewelry
to the oldest corner of the dark house
where rats are gnawing. Take cheese, five ounces,
preferably moldy, and write her name backwards
on a soft-shell crab. Eat it while farts
waft past that time-honored Szechuan dish,
the creamy casserole that made Susan ill.
Eat it by fistfuls, your stomach hers. Say:

Sour Cheerios and cesspool Smoothies, gray
chopmeat and the gums of old llamas.
May the double l's double over Susan.
May the pink of raw meat and mouth rip
her into puzzle pieces that tip
like a Rubic's Cube in the fat hands of God.

2.

When she denies she's flirting, slit open
a pepper and gather the seeds. Then spit
into a waiter's ear, eat rarebit
or Egg Foo Young, release doves. Now circle
her shoe which you've stolen, its purple
laces and lime-green sole. Take the tongue

of your ogling boss and, to the far-flung
noise of Nine-Inch Nails, wave it high and yell:

Goddess of Toe Nail Clippings and Bad Smells,
pluck Susan from each potential suitor
and stick her with a corsage pin saying: "For-
ever clumsy." May she wander dazed
through malls where she works for minimum wage
in stores where my lover would never shop.

3.

Razor the bristles off her wet toothbrush,
collect her saliva and plaque in a pouch.
Throw a carton of organic eggs, loud
and unfertilized, into her pancakes.
Now pee on a lamb's tongue then into a lake
where your power will do the most harm. Lick
the crispy raisin moles that dot your sick
mother's stomach and you're through. Ready? Say:

Goddess of Wheatgrass, keep Susan away
in the state of Kentucky where lovers
sleep in slop of pigs and fowl. May she hover
over the Jersey turnpike at rush hour
as she spends her years alone. May admirers
find her breath bad and her clitoris lax.

4.

Cull the sickest-looking fruit from the scarred bowl.
Mashing, drip something green from your mean face
into a stew of awkwardness and baste
until Susan is the shade of your eyebrows.
Stir until she is the shape of five cows—
never before has broth tasted so bossy!
Walk into a forest, bicycle or ski
where you can spin near wild mushrooms, singing:

47

May the angels toll for you, Susan, ring
creepy Alleluias into sex and dream.
May your days be dark and stained as red beets
as you crawl to find your dusty contact lens.
May the skinny ghost of Ichabod Crane
carry you, cashless, into K-Mart.

5.

Gather stereotypes who look like Susan.
Bring them, insipid and limp, to the cliff
where you saw her kiss your sweetheart. Don't mind if
the pain in her loins is stronger than rum.
Sing "Hey la hey la my girlfriend's back." Bum
a funny cigarette from a famous queen
whose danger is unknown. Sauté a cat's spleen,
if you can find one, and while you're cooking, say:

May the half-moons of your thumbnails slay
your future offspring, may their sharp white teeth
bite the TV cord during Ricki Lake week.
May safety pins leap through your ears and tongue
and lacerate you, Susan, the thin rungs
of your career plans ladder you into hell.

6.

Turn on the ceiling fan and imagine
her neck cut off by each whirring blade,
her spine collapsing like a blanched and frayed
embryo in the clinic's light. Pour urine
into the mouth of a north-flowing river
while drowning five blue newts in the creme bleach
she used to lighten her moustache. Eat
the dandruff you snatched from her collar. Holler:

May your leather be stolen at Girl Bar.
May your pee be green, may your hair be cut
by untrained stylists who highlight your bald spot.
May everyone who meets you say "Who?" May
you grow as lonely as rope. May you fly
into traffic begging my forgiveness.

7.

Now go to Penney's and hide in the smallest
dressing room until you see Susan's feet.
Stretch her toes until they resemble eels,
then bruise them with rocks or small furniture.
Take your brother's old odor-eaters,
the hair of a plucked nipple, and repeat.
Slip her photograph into a hive of bees
and as they sting her image, say out loud:

May you live to bowdlerize your proud
operas into fanny songs, your cinched
waistline into suet. May your rhinestoned hand
grow arthritic, and may your whiny voice
whine over the last prairie like a toy
airplane before it screams into flame and melts.

BABY DEMOCRATS

D—

I liked campaigning for Brenda Baker's father when he ran for
mayor—he was a Democrat and everyone poor loved him,
especially the folks in highrises who had nothing but their social
security checks. He sponsored pork and bean dinners for them,
right in the lobby of their buildings, and told them he'd protect
their social security forever and try to shorten the lines for public
housing. When you went door to door with those shiny flyers
and Mr. Baker's face you could tell right away who was a
Democrat. "A vote for Baker! A vote for change!" promised the
flyer and I believed it because people would call Mr. Baker at
home during supper and he'd take the call whoever it was, a
citizen complaining about a broken swing in the park, a divorcée
with no heat in her apartment. He'd let his mashed potatoes get
cold, then lumpy and hard while Brenda and her brothers and
sisters finished up and did the dishes. I thought Brenda was lucky
because every re-election year she was able to be in the papers,
her whole family dressed up and sitting in their living room
which was straightened up the day the photographer came.
Of course, Brenda saw her family's picture as an embarrassment
and hated politics. She was forced to carry the flyers to the
Republicans who slammed the door right in our faces, to the little
old ladies who bribed us to come in and sit down and talk about
Mayor Baker's campaign over Fig Newtons and brownies. There
were dogs that scared us and people who worked third shift who
we'd woken up by ringing their bells who would chase us away,
calling us little shits. And I felt bad every time that happened,

that we'd lost a vote for Mayor Baker who would make sure more kids got free hot lunches, who would make sure the nursery schools were safe and had lots of toys. I liked the buttons we wore that said Baker, the cheese Danish in the Democrat's office downtown that was converted to Santa's house right after the election was over.

M—

Adlai was a sacred name, I said it like Jesus, almost with a sign of the cross on my forehead, chest, and shoulders or with a bow of my head. He even looked like Jesus to me and when he lost it was Good Friday all over again and my family mourned, everything was purple for days and there was no resurrection, it was more like a simple flush of the toilet and the Democrats were gone. The '50s were pastel years, only computer chips budded in the basements, the rest of America sailed in the sunshine. We feared bombs, yes, wasn't someone supposed to get even with us for something? But basically, we were pink and aqua and flamingos and Disneyland. Last week my father said it had been a mistake for him to move our family to Connecticut in '58. It was the first time I ever heard him use the "m" word and I paused over the German meal he'd bought for us because he had a taste for schnitzel. He still looks like Adlai, I said to myself, swallowing something gluey and strong, a liver dumpling, a forty-year-old bone—he looks like Jesus, the thinning black-Irish hair, the strong Semitic snout.

D—

I don't remember where I was when Kennedy was shot since I was only two, but my mother says that she was sobbing on the couch, watching the black and white TV, crisscrossing the bunny ears to get the picture clearer, hoping that by moving the antenna she could make the horror go away, that maybe she was just getting a dream station or a station from outer space. I was two and my sister had just been born and she claims that like always I wanted her attention and this time she just couldn't give it to me, her grief as big as Canada or maybe the whole globe itself. Maybe she thought about whether she should call one of her sisters. I was toilet-trained but I stood in front of her trying to block the TV, defiant, and peed into the carpet. For Democrats, responsibility to Kennedy was bigger than responsibility to your own family. Aunt Bea had an 8 1/2 by 11 of Kennedy, framed in the same frames as Jesus and her sons. She braided palms she got from the church on Palm Sunday and put them around Kennedy's picture to protect his soul. She said after Kennedy was shot, nothing else would be good and I wished I could remember my country, those first two years of my life, that Democratic Catholic hope, that pre-Marilyn scandal, pre-Chappaquiddick time, that Cape Cod love, those pillbox hats and neatness.

M—

My father was always a Democrat and my mother went along. When he switched in the Reagan years she followed like his favorite lamb and they marched into their future, true gold-street Americans ready to live out the dream. I'm not sure how money changes you, why you suddenly need it so much more one day than you did the day before or why the idea that you've earned it means it's more precious than something else, like play time. I get confused that Wall Street exists, and people in huge houses along the lakeshore, along the rivers, flush against the oceans like dams holding back the flood. When my father was a drinking man he brought home an African diplomat he'd met in a bar to join our family for Sunday dinner. It was the Kennedy years, hope flew, it was the tender age, we were all school children, even the oldest of us, we all pretended that good would win, no one smelled the word: hypocrisy. The diplomat ate my mother's beef and Yorkshire pudding, he liked my father, you could see how they lifted their glasses and toasted each other's liberty. My mother was so pretty, she looked exactly like Jackie Kennedy, thin and large-eyed. One of my sisters was born the same month as little John. The country was a happy baby, our family a tiny mouth, gurgling through ice cream.

D—

I was in high school when Watergate happened, when my father said, "Don't blame me, I didn't vote for him" and my mother said,

"They all do it—he was just the one who got caught." And my uncle took my sister and me to the Smithsonian where I wore a sweater so pale pink people mistook it for white. The color was like a blush, the embarrassment at my breasts which seemed bigger than any of my friends' at school, the embarrassment of believing in politics, of being wide-eyed and naive, for running for student council and trying to get our class to go to Diamond Hill and pick up the trash, for volunteering through the CYO to take care of retarded kids on the weekends, for writing to Senator Claiborne Pell about the the hazard of spray cans to the ozone layer. I was a chump, a sucker. My uncle drove us towards Watergate trying to point out the right floor and we circled it, and I was surprised to learn that Watergate was simply the name of a hotel. I thought it was something ominous and bigger, like a passage to hell or a button that could potentially blow up the world. Even though I watched the hearings every afternoon, the hearings that pre-empted *Dark Shadows*, I never heard anyone say Watergate was a hotel, a round one with balconies near the Pentagon which I thought sounded strangely like pentagram which reminded me of movies with devil-worshipers and symbols so scary that if you paint them in your attic they can burn your house down. Now politics was evil, and Terry Malois was caught fixing the student council vote because at our school you counted the ballots by hand. And the voting booth looked strangely like a confessional, nothing else quite so private and sacred in America and I imagined the jaded, the ones who knew everyone deep down was a crook, that even the most moral had a price, the ones who had bumper stickers that read "Look out for Number One!" I imagined them in those booths doing unthinkable things, like spitting on all the levers and peeing in the corners.

M—

I got to vote at exactly eighteen, but McGovern lost, and the next time I was having a baby and didn't know about absentee ballots, four years could sneak up on you like that, and nothing ever changed anyway. There I was, one of those Americans you hear about drifting unceremoniously into apathy. This is what apathy feels like: gradual sinking, slipping down the mud, never a bottom, no foothold, it has to do with reaching in your pocket, there's a token and a wad of lint, your baby's got an ugly rash on her butt and and it's a choice between Desitin and milk. When my mother was nominated for the Daughters of the American Revolution and my dad bought his first Cadillac, I stood still in my life and looked around. My young Wall Street husband beckoned from the Plaza Hotel, we were on our way to Delmonicos, the baby pressed in organdy for Christmas, my bubble waited like a transformed pumpkin with transformed mice at the curb of affluence and influence and some richer calling I didn't hear. The bubble that would ride me to the tower where the family at the end of the gem-encrusted street would take me into their arms and rock me to sleep.

EXQUISITE COMMUNIST

Their world is red banners and small potatoes,
soft rotten ones sprouting eyes.
Doctors and plumbers are paid the same
as dogwalkers. Everyone wears brown and loden green.
Even the children blossom in shades of tan.
The sky is a gray metal file cabinet,
the stars full of spy secrets.
Once the tallest building in the Bronx
was the Russian building. It leaned as the government leaned
into China or Vietnam. The computers were big
and old and not very good, statues the color of mold,
their genitals shrunken, frozen, sorrowful.
There is one Communist left in New York City. Her name is Sam
and she would prefer it if you gave your leftovers
to the neighbors. If she were president
someone would probably murder her instantly,
in her sleep, and she'd never get media coverage.
I did my eighth grade social studies report on Communism.
I liked the ideas, though I never got around to becoming one.

BEACH BUNNIES

VENUS CLAMS (VENERIDAE) ARE PROBABLY THE MOST SUCCESSFUL OF ALL THE CLAMS. OVER 400 ABUNDANT SPECIES OCCUR THE WORLD OVER. A FLEXIBLE EXTERNAL LIGAMENT AND A POWERFUL MUSCLE ATTACHED TO THE INTERIOR OF THE SHELLS ENABLE THE ANIMAL TO OPEN ITS VALVES AND CLOSE THEM TO PROTECT ITS SOFT BODY.
—FROM SEASHELLS IN MY POCKET

1. *King Venus* (Southern Florida to the West Indies)

She's a wet-sand wallower, a sucker
for surfers named Tulip and Sweet Limpid,
her boogie board, slick with sea foam that hints
of underwater sex. Even the straight
mollusks rip off their goggles to watch her bait
deep-sea hooks, snag starfish, throw them back in
and head for McDonald's. King's father's grin
was hers, even before her first bright tooth
bloomed above water. At night she's aloof,
pensive, a bruise in the sand, a figment
of her own detachment. King's spotted pigment
is hardly the envy of most Venuses
who prefer seaweed soup and real penises.
Silly clams. Only the Queen gets to fuck her.

2. *Elegant Venus* (Texas to the Caribbean)

This princess prefers silly clams around her
to out-of-reach-deep-sea types who dress
in green-thread algae. Elegant spends less
on clothes than...no one, come to think of it,
not even the glamorous Textile Cone, twit-
of-the-sea, not even tiny Pertusa.
Elegant is luscious wet. To lose her
would bring Mister Venus to the foamy edge
of her bristly purple shell. Uncaged,
she gulps down enough ocean for a bath,
enough sand for pearly intestines. Paths
all lead to Elegant, her soft body
a percussion of undertow, muddy,
delirious as the sea's fickle weather.

3. *Lightning Venus* (North Carolina to Brazil)

Crazy about delirious weather,
Lightning creates a good storm. Thunder booms,
typically, and she precedes it—zoom,
zap, cutting close to her lover's bones.
She aches, pulled palp and muscles, electric moans
that curl dulse leaves and tough eel grass.
Once she smoked an entire avalanche
of sea potatoes. It's her specialty:
beach peas, wrinkled rose, and link confetti
flash fried, a potion that works every time,
deadly as ink blood of octopi. Briny
ghosts follow Lightning's phosphorescent foot,
her shadowy imprint, her haloed hood—
the flash of her push, the flash of her lure.

4. *Golden Venus* (Philippines and East Asia)

One flashy mama, a pushy crone clam,
reef-famous Golden holds her own among
whipper-snappers, rappers and slackers, young
upstarts. Golden loves the sea when it's gray,
rusty treasure off the coast of Asia,
tilted ships pining on the ocean floor.
She's seen entire shorelines shift, sea wars,
and giant tourists in green water-wings
floating to paradise. Golden careens
down Ocean Boulevard like a pelican
on rollerblades, hungry and determined.
She hates being called ma'am, "Loving Care
Silver" all she ever uses on her hair,
the color of neap tides, dazzling star-streaked sand.

5. *Lettered Venus* (Indo-Pacific)

Her dazzling studies claim stars control tongues
and tides—*not* man or moon. Shocked academics
speculate about her bold linguistic
powers, wonder if her words predate God-
babble: the Koran, Torah, St. James, odd
holy books that read like dark fairy tales.
One day she woke with the lyrics of whales
imprinted on her back—their brackish mumblings,
disgruntled or ecstatic etched rumbles.
Anywhere words have been swallowed by the sea
she carries history, her body a key
to salty laws and knowledge that swells
from carp livers and the aortas of eels,
from the swordfish's sword, the lungfish's lung.

6. *Pointed Venus* (southern Florida, Texas, Mexico)

Pointed's got that sword-to-the-lung attitude.
Addicted to bivalve adrenalin,
she power-lunches with crestfallen
Sanguin Clams, gives them no-nonsense peptalks
re: *clam* defense, *clam*ouflage, and walking
like a *clam*-man. Pointed is all mer-woman,
fin-sharp and liquid, a lover of lumin-
ous debate. Once she fought off a whole school
of pacifists, detonating peace symbols
in the Gulf of Mexico. Pointed
wants to go where no Venus has gone—join
the Volutes in West Africa, pilgrimage
up the Mississippi to the edge
of fresh water, lethal ponds, forbidden food.

7. *Glory-of-the-Seas Venus* (North Carolina to Texas)

She's the Mother of Ponds, slick forbidden
deep-water siren who sings you to death
with her dolphin-inspired crystal-meth
melodies. Venuses worship her fluent
fluid ideas about valve-control, the Ten
Glorious Suggestions, earning her a place
of saint-like stardom in offshore bass-
holy waters. Glory is not only
Diva of the Deep, Bivalve Supreme, Roaring
Pink-Mouthed Queen, and Patron Saint of Pismos,
but she also conjures cures for dismal
beaches. She purifies polluted oceans,
tweaking the little toes of humans
who wallow in the wet sand sucking up clams.

LITANY OF THE FATHERS

An indulgence of 7 years. A plenary indulgence once a month under the usual conditions if this Litany is recited daily.

Father of lawn mowers and rakes, *we demand you hear us*
Father of belches and Superbowls, *deliver now*
Father most injurious, father of secrets and shame, father of white
   lies and tax evasion, *pay us back*

Father at the bottom of the stairs yelling, "Get down here,"
   pay us back
Father who left us, father who stayed behind but never said
   a word, *pay us back*
Father who taught *nigger, faggot, bitch,* father who farted and
   laughed, *pay us back*
Father on the toilet reading *Playboy, pay us back*
Father tickling his child to inconstancy, *pay us back*
Father of suburban household, leaving early, getting home late,
   pay us back
Father playing lotto, *pay us back*
Disowning father of the pregnant bride, *pay us back*
Father who has nothing to say when his grown kids call,
   pay us back
Dilatory father, father of cocaine and drug busts, *pay us back*
Father of stress and high blood pressure, *pay us back*
Bartender father, keeper of the booze, *pay us back*
Father of the American flag tattoo, *pay us back*

Father of shit-stained boxers and Listerine, *pay us back*
Father of odoreaters and athlete's foot, *pay us back*
Father of jock itch and joust, *pay us back*
Father who says he couldn't care less, *pay us back*
Father who makes fun of his daughter's new breasts, *pay us back*
Father who screams "Put on your robe," *pay us back*

All you bearded keepers of ships and lighthouses, *hear us*
Sweepers of schools, molesters of 4th graders, *hear us*
Watchers of hockey and stripteases, *hear us*
Translators of Wall Street, runners of numbers, *hear us*
Betters and winners, *hear us*
Catcallers and those who expose themselves at bus stops,
    hear us
All you slumlords and lords of Saturday night poker, *hear us*
University deans and porn collectors, *hear us*
Shoe salesmen and early morning rapists, *hear us*
Innuendo experts, flirtatious heads of English Departments,
    hear us
Golf pros, *hear us*
All you war makers and exploitive art collectors, *hear us*
Astronauts and pilots, *hear us*
Pool cleaners and the makers of TV sitcoms, *hear us*
Connoisseurs of hops and Marlboros, *hear us*
Connoisseurs of pussy and tit, *hear us*
Varicosed droolers who marry eighteen-year-old girls, *hear us*
Tellers of bad jokes, players of dominoes, *hear us*
Funny little snorers in dark movie theaters, *hear us*
Mail-order bride buyers, *hear us*
Hunters of small game, hunters of big game, *hear us*
Grunters and truck drivers, *hear us*
Belittling doctors and dentists, *hear us*
Doctors and dentists who demand immediate payment, *hear us*
Car mechanics who overcharge and look down blouses, *hear us*
Cat haters and ball adjusters, *hear us*

Motherfucker most violent, *leave us alone*
Motherfucker of no counsel, *leave us alone*
Motherfucker most unmerciful, *leave us alone*

Motherfucker most unfaithful, *leave us alone*
Motherfucker who covets virgins, *leave us alone*
Motherfucker most impatient, *leave us alone*
Cheap motherfucker, *leave us alone*
Motherfucker most demanding of obedience, *leave us alone*
Motherfucker, model of vice, *leave us alone*
Motherfucker, power player, *leave us alone*
Motherfucker, treasure keeper, *leave us alone*
Motherfucker, teacher of greed, *leave us alone*
Motherfucker, author of lies, *leave us alone*
Motherfucker, our brother, *leave us alone*
Motherfucker, our lover, *leave us alone*

Vague prop, *grant us our just rewards*
Parody of Popeye, *grant us our just rewards*
Vessel of unwanted children, *grant us our just rewards*
Redundancy, *grant us our just rewards*
Tower of authority and speeding tickets, *grant us our
    just rewards*
Tower of ivory towers, *grant us our just rewards*
Tower of canon, *grant us our just rewards*
House of smashed-in walls, *grant us our just rewards*
Rod and reel, *grant us our just rewards*
Refuge for no one, *grant us our just rewards*
Health for the rich, *grant us our just rewards*
King of clipboards and middle management, *grant us
    our just rewards*
King of expansion and colonialism, *grant us our just rewards*
King of inexpensive cologne, *grant us our just rewards*
King of gold chains, *grant us our just rewards*
Handcuff King, Lazy-Boy King, *grant us our just rewards*
King of dirty socks and overflowing hamper, *grant us
    our just rewards*
King of long-winded introductions, *grant us our just rewards*
TV Candy King, *grant us our just rewards*
King of tool belts and hot rods, *grant us our just rewards*
King of Boardwalk and Park Place, *grant us our just rewards*
Hard core King, hard hat King, *grant us our just rewards*

King of Warner Brothers and Barnes & Noble, *grant us
    our just rewards*
King of Christians and Jews, *grant us our just rewards*
King of embryos, *grant us our just rewards*
King of decision and entertainment, *grant us our just rewards*
King of the confessional, *grant us our just rewards*

Through your Swiss bank accounts, *deliver now*
Through your memory of being teased on the playground,
    deliver now
Through your memory of the day your first pet died, *deliver now*
Through Raisinettes and Jujubes, *deliver now*
Through the gums under your false teeth, *deliver now*
Through your sensitive nipples, *deliver now*
Through your need for hair transplants, *deliver now*
Through your love handles and pot bellies, *deliver now*
Through your prostrate problems, *deliver now*
Through your stutter to find the right word, *deliver now*
Through your inability to be lost, *deliver now*
Through your inability to ask directions, *deliver now*
Through your drug rehabilitation, *deliver now*
Through your frightened will and testimony, *deliver now*
Through your sleep when you are most harmless, *deliver now*
Through your crutches and eye patch, *deliver now*
Through your inability to hold back orgasm, *deliver now*
Through your war wounds, *deliver now*

That you would step down as senators, *we demand you hear us*
That you would plant new trees, *we demand you hear us*
That you would share your marbles, *we demand you hear us*
That you would let another drive the car while you sit
    in the passenger seat, *we demand you hear us*
That you would not feel threatened by your children's anger,
    we demand you hear us
That you would not walk away when others are talking,
    we demand you hear us
That you would visit your child's school on report card day,
    we demand you hear us

That you would come home kind from work, *we demand you hear us*

That you would get off the train sober, *we demand you hear us*

That you would stay in the delivery room, *we demand you hear us*

That you would not leave when the subjects of pregnancy or periods come up and you would stay in your chair until the heat of your blush makes you wise, *we demand you hear us*

Let us pray

Almighty and eternal God, look upon the hearts of your beloved sons and grant forgiveness. *Amen.*

ECOFEMINISM IN THE YEAR 2000

1. The Beast

Love, I bought you a chunk of the rainforest, now what?
Will the blind bird in the middle of all that green speak,

trust us as foster mom and pop? The mist of London,
captive in the violet of your eyelashes, suggests

not. The sad loops in your sad leopard activist coat.
You were the one the wolves adopted when your father

left to develop his chain of theme parks, his fortune
in this glut of global poverty a sober sum.

I've rejected all blood types not my own just to have
five hairy offspring with their taste for Brazilian tea.

As if a man knew how to nurse, I sang to the moon,
mornings, when the last feral child left for preschool,

the plaid satchels and lunch boxes we bestowed upon
female and male alike glinting in the undertow.

Family to each radioactive morsel, we speak
the same holographic syllables the earth murmurs:

Can natural women cast unnatural shadows?
Will the scraping of wind on stone provide enough sound?

The realigned shorelines, the sad sighs of seismographs
never topped the drama of your dolphin fleet aiming

kisses toward the false promise of mistletoe sprigs,
then dropping one by one to the continental shelf

mislabeled flasks: battle-war-poisonous gas-water.
When our eldest was born, she rocked like an old woman.

Our shadows are not the only doubles. Multiple
rings around the moon portend mayhem, a rash of tides

undrinkably dry, unbeatable triplets, chaos
in the ova of newborns, seed fluorescent, quiet

jellyfish suctioned to the night sky. Oh what mirrors
the eerie eyes of children! The rainforest steams, Love.

We've isolated each vapor, and still, no answer
to the blind bird's fervent silence, the feral child's sleep.

Who can dream such breezes able to cure diseased wings?
The rainforest's gnarled taproot nurtures beauty and beast.

2. Beauty

If I had as many children as I have fingers,
and the lynx moved gracefully through snow, leading deeper

into each bombed-out capital, I'd still have these aches,
the purity of grief after loving. Now winter

is more humid than ever. The Beast fixes the fan
while the child caught in puberty glistens in half-light.

Not quite boy or girl, Feral longs for separation
from unrecognizable siblings who blindly suck

their own webbed thumbs for comfort. Once, telekinesis
was peculiar to the Temperate Zone, to bald mutants

who knew only push-pins on maps. When East shifted West,
I was struck by a shoe of Bulgarian leather.

I fought back, hurling color TVs at war generals,
microwave ovens at Wall Street types. I was lovely

crossing enemy lines without lifting a finger.
Like Venus unclothed, I lulled the hungry border guards

who up until now had scoffed at the surge of white witches
and lapsed Baptists with cowrie shells in their coiled black hair.

With eyes for life, we'd voted to save each frog and bug.
Our children held hands across the fishless Pacific,

and the hysterectomy scars of the world's highways
faded into translucence like a woman dying.

Imagine, I'm the only one purely feminine,
purely masculine, lupine, stunned by a meteor

that swirled my sexes together in fallout shelters.
Who tells futures without sight? Gives birth without a womb

or breasts? It was not enough to fire old language, hire
every skilled princess, every global architect's wife.

We learned history as we taught, pointers to chalkboards
and constellations that changed shape as the earth evolved.

Each cancer cell healed itself after so much dark,
each isotope, radiant in the designs of men—

politicians' hallucinations or dynamos
generating child from ash, woman from untold night.

3. The Feral Child

When I put my ear to the conch shell, I hear bullets—
as if the ocean's violence could end in a muzzle.

My legacy leaves me small and sadly wise, toothaches
from lost shrapnel in my jaw, mindless, American

scholar: North Central South. Like Beauty and Beast in me,
the planet came together beneath mushrooms of light.

I remember my birth clearly: a slow-flying fish
from a frightened mother panting to keep me inside

her sea. "The child's strong enough for air," the midwife said,
but the air was blood, and as I suckled the new world

I tasted contamination. Sunset—colored rust,
streaked with skywritings of my birth—would soon be extinct

along with saplings exhibited in museums.
This is my fear: That in loving I'll bequeath evil,

that in dying I'll leave no message of hope. Childhood
forces me to play, to laugh, to question the absurd.

Our curio cabinet boasts a rain forest chunk
of steamy black earth, a bird the ancient blue of sky

but as small as a postmodern atom. Each theory
of survival, each trout fisher and dealer of war

concocted a nursery rhyme excuse. Bullies all,
smug keepers of fire and keys proven wrong—I exist!

though sterility hampers my claiming so. Future
issues of *Bride* and *Essence* no longer tantalize

their target groups. There's little money in making guns
now that no one's left to kill, no neighbors to covet

in traditional ways. Green means kill and black means change.
But where does a child who's lost the moon begin? Beauty

blessed me with her strength though few verbs remain.
  I'm happy
as a disc jockey of survival sounds, as the Beast

when he's busy. Knowing no other world, I absolve
every sibling's sin, every soiled day's beginning.

Tomorrow tumbles backwards then forwards then sideways
into a light I believe ineluctably mine.

EXQUISITE POLITICS

The perfect voter has a smile but no eyes,
maybe not even a nose or hair on his or her toes,
maybe not even a single sperm cell, ovum, little paramecium.
Politics is a slug copulating in a Poughkeepsie garden.
Politics is a grain of rice stuck in the mouth
of a king. I voted for a clump of cells,
anything to believe in, true as rain, sure as red wheat.
I carried my ballots around like smokes, pondered big questions,
resources and need, stars and planets, prehistoric
languages. I sat on Alice's mushroom in Central Park,
smoked longingly in the direction of the mayor's mansion.
Someday I won't politic anymore, my big heart will stop
loving America and I'll leave her as easy as a marriage,
splitting our assets, hoping to get the advantage
before the other side yells: *Wow!* America,
Vespucci's first name and home of free and brave, *Te amo.*

ABOUT THE AUTHORS

Denise Duhamel is the author of four books of poems: *Kinky* (Orchises Press, 1997); *Girl Soldier* (Garden Street Press, 1996); *The Woman with Two Vaginas* (Salmon Run Press, 1995), winner of the Salmon Run Poetry Prize; and *Smile!* (Warm Spring Press, 1993) She is the recipient of a 1989 New York Foundation for the Arts Fellowship and the winner of a Poets & Writers "Writers Exchange" Award. Her work has been published in magazines such as *The American Poetry Review, Partisan Review,* and *Ontario Review,* and in anthologies including *Best American Poetry* 1993 and 1994.

Maureen Seaton's poetry collections are: *Furious Cooking* (University of Iowa Press, 1996), winner of the Iowa Prize and the Lambda Award; *The Sea among the Cupboards* (New Rivers, 1992), winner of the Capricorn Award and the Society of Midland Authors Award; and *Fear of Subways* (The Eighth Mountain Press, 1991), winner of The Eighth Mountain Poetry Prize. She was the recipient in 1994 of an NEA fellowship and an Illinois Arts Council grant. Her poems have appeared in *The Atlantic, The Paris Review, The New Republic, The Pushcart Prize* XX and XXII, *Best American Poetry* 1997, and other publications.